C000001102

Intoxicated Minds

JADE MILLARD

leaf
publishing
house

Trigger Warning

The contents of this book could be triggering for some people.

Discretion is highly advised.

Foreword

Dearest reader,

Throughout both my childhood and adolescence, writing has always been the one thing that has stayed with me. I've never felt particularly skilled, but I know in my heart that I've always excelled in reading and writing. My main ambition in life is to help others, and have a strong, positive impact on the lives of young people especially. If I take both of these passions, and put them together, that's how 'Intoxicated Minds' was born. The first time I wrote a poem was in a Citizenship class back when I was 12 years old, and that very piece can be found in the 2nd chapter of this book, under the title 'Abandoned Aged 6'. I have been writing them ever since then, as a coping mechanism for whatever life has thrown at me.

Growing up is far from easy, and for me personally, it's been a turbulent ride. I've experienced certain events that I never even imagined would become my reality, and I've crumbled and cried in my room on so many dark, lonely nights. I've encountered people, who have almost shattered me to the core, and I've also spent years supporting those who have sometimes ended up unexpectedly toxic.

I've now made it to the age of 18, and I'm ready to share my story with the world. Some of these poems will tug at your heart-strings, some of them will have you nodding along in agreement, and others will make you feel as strong and as sassy as you should always feel. At least that's what I'm hoping for!

These pages genuinely are home to so many of the thoughts, and emotions that have been present in my life throughout the years and I've had to bare my soul and make myself vulnerable in order to share them with billions of strangers.

Writing has quite honestly made me the person that I am today, and the person that I'm becoming. It has allowed me to speak my mind, it has encouraged me to be open with myself, it has provided me with a way to ramble, and it has guided me through the trauma that I have had to endure.

I hope that this book helps you in the same way that it has helped me. I want you to cherish it, wear the pages out with your fingertips, your tears and your fluorescent highlighters, hold it lovingly like a comfort blanket on every occasion that you feel alone, and find sanity in the idea that you're connecting with a soul sister. Treat it like a treasured possession, and take it with you throughout all of the trials and tribulations that come your way during your youth.

Myself, and 'Intoxicated Minds' will be there for you when your absent father isn't, when you're being bullied, when you get your heart broken for the first time, when you lose your group of girlfriends, and when you can't figure out who you are as an individual, even though you are all you have got. We will equally be there for you when the sun is shining, and you're living your best life at the end of this battle.

Thank you to every single person who picks up a copy, and who reads my words in their purest state. It means more to me than you will ever know, and from the day I hold this book in my hand, I'm forever grateful.

All my love,
Jade.

Contents

1
Enlighten

Relying On Romance

Do not rely on romance to keep you alive
Do not rely on love to keep your spirits high
Some potential love interests will come and
some will go
You just have to keep staying strong
Do not cling too tightly on
Before you realise,
(S)he may walk out (S)he may break your heart in two
Do not give him/her that power
Do not give him/her that control
If (s)he wants to be in your life,
(s)he will prove it to you
Before you realise it, you will grow old
So, do not allow a boy/girl to put your life on hold.

How To Be Kind

You should wake up with a positive attitude
Think about your goals for the day
Remind yourself that
no matter what happens
It will all be okay
You may make some new friends
Talk to them until your heart's content
Ask them what they have been up to
They may be feeling as though they cannot
go on and stay strong
Pick some flowers for your Mum
Help an elderly person to carry their bags
Just do a good deed,
as you have nothing to lose
It may turn out to be rewarding,
if not fun
Always think about how others feel
Be there for them in their times of need.

Saving Yourself

The reality of it is
There is not always going to be people to save you
Sometimes,
you just have to save yourself.

"Falling" In Love Ends In Disaster

Love is quite literally a black hole
When you are metaphorically falling for someone
It all seems so romanticised
So airy fairy and carefree
Your eyes are only attracted to the one that you desire
Yet when you have reached your chosen
destination of a lover
Nothing is quite as it initially seemed
You are tumbling down the black hole
Head first with absolutely no control
This is why you should not 'fall' in love
As you will only ever crash and burn.

Smile Through The Sadness

Not everybody will like you
Not everybody will understand you
Not everybody will treat you as if
you are somebody
All of that is irrelevant
You need to be aware of your self-worth
You need to radiate positivity
You need to smile through the sadness
Anything is possible
and
you can do whatever your heart desires.

Heal Or Harm

Words can either heal the soul
Or harm the soul
They can either make a person's day
Or break apart a person's day.

Not Everybody Will Stay

People will come and people will go
That is something out of your control
How they impacted your life will
always stay with you though
The way they made their exit will forever
remain in your soul
It will either fill you with relief or crush you to the bone.

Do Not Believe That Your Future Is Bleak

People will come and people will go
This will happen many times in a row
Do not let it dampen your spirits
or
make you feel weak
It does not mean that your entire life is bleak
Just because someone does not stick around
It does not mean that your soulmate cannot be found
Someday,
someone will look at you as though you put
the stars in the sky
Then you will finally realise that
 you are worthy of love
 and
the reason(s) why.

You Are Perfectly Whole On Your Own

You were whole before (s)he came into your life
And you will continue to remain whole
long after (s)he's gone
You are not a puzzle
You do not need a (wo)man to fit in the missing piece of
your life
That is not how it works
You are your own person
No (wo)man or relationship symbolises your worth.

Your Lover Should Find You A Pleasure

Exposing yourself to someone else is never easy
I am not going to refer to it as a 'task'
As it is not something that you should feel the need to
tick off your to do list
It is not a set requirement
Yet,
it is still just as difficult when
it is an option
The person you are making love to does not own you
They never have
and
they never will
Your body can only be admired
Not edited by a significant other and their opinions
They can choose to admire the masterpiece in front of
them
Or they can encourage you to save the art you have
created
for that special someone
Who will pay it all their attention
out of the thousands of paintings in the gallery
that they could have chosen from.

Do Not Lower Your Volume

Ever since the day you were born,
you have had a purpose
And you will continue to have one until
the day you die
Nobody can put out that fire inside of you
It is a part of your identity
Your passion is what keeps you going each day
That is something that nobody can ever steal from you
You were created with a burning fire in your soul
You were born to roar out loud for what is right.

Do Not Push Someone To The Edge

You thoughtless piece of shit
Your words hurt more than a hit
Do you not understand how you made me feel?
The pain is now just too real
I do not know what you get out of making someone fret
You are not cool,
clever,
funny,
or
big
You are instead incredibly nasty,
and
stupid
Think about what you say before you express
your thoughts
As your hurtful words could push someone to
turn into a corpse
Just have a little more consideration for others
instead of yourself
It really is no good for their mental health
Spread love and positivity,
not hatred and negativity.

They Are Worthy If They Wait

If they are worth it,
they will wait
You need to recognise whether it is
a mistake or fate
Do not just do what pleases them
You should only expect someone who is
a true gem
Remember that your body is a work of art
Only show it to those who respect you from the start.

People Do Not Always Keep Promises

You cannot keep going back to the human
that you once called your home
Sometimes,
you just have to try and seek happiness
on your own
Even when people promise you forever
They do not always mean that they will
be there for you through whatever
It is important to have your own back
and put your mental health first.

Consider Your Purpose

Do not make someone your everything
As once they are gone,
you will feel like you are worth nothing
They will take everything that you have and more
But,
be just as quick to walk out of the door
You need to recognise your own worth
Think about what your purpose is on this Earth.

The Idea Of Being Together Forever

You do not want to move on,
do you?
He said that you would be together forever
He promised that he would never leave your side,
not even for a day
He swore to you that he would always stay
Yet,
You were forced to let go of his destructive, unfaithful
ways
You were persuaded into leaving him
Maybe the people who were encouraging you had a
reason?
Maybe,
just maybe
they were right?
All he did was lie to you
and break your beautiful being apart into
tiny
little
fragments
You have always been a sensitive soul,
right from the very start
Yet

now,
you are even more sensitive
Now that you are apart
You are having to let go of the one person
you loved most
The one you thought would never leave
The one you thought you would always have
It really does go to show that sometimes
Things just are not meant to be.

You Are A Diamond In Disguise

Not everyone is going to acknowledge and appreciate
your worth
You are a diamond in disguise
Yet others often mistake you for a rock
They only see your insecurities
They do not take the time to admire you
You are a work of art
You are an award-winning masterpiece
One day,
you will find the right people
You will find those who admire you
You will find those who take time to explore you
It will all be worth it in the end.

Morphing Into One

Relationships can often absorb your identity
You can end up morphing into your significant other
without even realising
That is the way they gain their control
They know that once the both of you have become one
You have nowhere left to run
No way of undoing what has been done
They have full power
They have full control over your mind,
your body
and
your soul.

You Are The One To Blame

Can you not see what this pain is doing to me?
It is causing endless self-destruction
Complete and utter misery
I do not know how much more I can bear
You all seem so unaware,
like you simply do not care
My emotions are like fire
they are unable to handle calmly
once they start spewing
If only you knew what you were
so selfishly doing
When I am not smiling anymore
Don't you dare put me to blame
You should be the ones feeling guilt and shame.

People Can Become A Master In Lying

When you love someone,
your vision can often become blurred
That is something that I have experienced first-hand,
and also heard
You cannot see how toxic they are
They are the one you wish for every time you
look up above and see a star
All you are aware of is their seemingly
good heart
Little do you know that they have mastered lying
as if it is an art.

Letting Go Is Always The Hardest Part

It is so hard to let go of a past lover
You have to find a whole other person to discover
The memories of your relationship will not just
automatically disappear from your mind
As all you ever seem to think about is going back
in time
by
pressing rewind
Putting on a brave face
and
attempting to stay strong are the
two things that seem
impossible
But
they are vital if you are to have any hope
in ever moving on.

Words Of Wisdom

If I could give you one bit of advice,
right here,
right now.
I would tell you to never give up on the thing(s) that
makes you feel alive
Even if people belittle you based upon your beliefs,
Or they disown you for whatever it may be that you
dream of
Do not let that stop you from doing everything in your
power to pursue your passions
People are not always permanent,
especially when you are younger,
and going through your teenage years
But,
your dreams can become a reality,
and they can take you further than any
temporary friend ever could.

Devoted Until Death

As much as this truth may hurt you
It is imperative that you remember it
If someone does not want to be saved
You will not be able to save them
No matter how much time and love you put in.

One Day, You Will Not Remember Their Name

There is going to be at least one human in your life that
will break you
Whenever you are alone at night,
you will shatter once more
And this will happen
again
and
again
and
again
You will see him/her around school or college
and you will be stabbed in the heart
once more,
just like you were the day before
He/she will tell you that he/she is in love
with another boy/girl
And when you hear that statement,
your head will begin to whirl
When you are on your own,
let all of these emotions out
Scream,
cry,
punch a pillow,

open your windows

and

shout

It is absolutely normal

and totally okay to

feel this way

Once you feel free of your fury,

focus on the next brand-new day

Wipe your enchanting eyes

and lift your head up high like you own it

Do not show your ex-lover that you ever even

gave a single shit

You are worth a million times more than this

And I can assure you,

eventually,

he/she will not even be missed.

For My Future Son Or Daughter

My baby,
If ever you need anything from me
Please do not ever hesitate to ask
Whether it is 1pm
or
4am
You will never be bothering me
You do not need to turn to
strangers on Snapchat for solace
You do not need to
dabble in drugs with a
dodgy dealer in a
random alley as
a way of getting adequate attention
Text me,
call me,
come to me
Whether you are a matter of minutes old
or
70 years old
I will hold you
until your anxieties have been laid to rest
I will stroke your hair

and
I will tell you that
everything will be okay
If you need to take a day off school for your mental
health,
I understand
I will stay with you
until a smile starts to form in the corners of your mouth
I will feed you cookie dough ice cream and
listen to you talk about your thoughts
If ever you feel the desire to reach for that razor
I beg you do the opposite of what I did,
Walk right away from it
You are so much more than self-inflicting scars
When I was a teenager,
I turned to self-destructive behaviours
I will not allow the same to happen with
my precious child
Whether I have 1, 2, 3, 4
or
even more
I looked for love in all of the wrong places and
all of the wrong people
You play a massive part in the reason as to why
I am still here today

Writing this letter for you

We will get through all of your battles together,

I promise you now,

as your Mother

I will never turn a blind eye to your cries for help

You will crumble many times throughout your teenage years

And probably after that too

But for each time your knees begin to weaken

I will be right beside you,

teaching you to rise

and

rise

again

Just like I have been doing all this time

On my own.

2
Empathise

Abandoned Aged 6

When I found out you left,
I felt a sharp pain in my chest
How could you do this
With such short notice?
I barely even knew what was happening
I was so young
Relying on Mum
to share all of that childhood fun
Nothing was heard for years
Meanwhile,
I was shedding many tears
That is all I have to say
Maybe one day,
someday
You will come back into my life again
And stay.

Aiming Towards The Bright Light

No matter how much you may be struggling now
I promise you,
there is a light at the end of the tunnel
There is hope,
even in the darkest of times
When everything seems to be going wrong
And nothing seems to be going right
Hold onto hope and aim towards that light
The one in the distance that is shining oh so bright
You will make it through,
I promise you
Just do what you have to do
In order to become the very best version of you.

Caught Up In Your Spell

I like to refer to love as a black hole
You dragged me right into it without preparing me at all
I had no idea how badly I would fall
You had me caught up in a spell
It felt like heaven at the time,
but maybe it was actually hell
I was completely and utterly blind
As you were the only thing that was on my mind.

Heartbreak Hurts

We did not have an ordinary love
For the majority of our relationship
It felt as though I was fighting a losing battle
I was holding onto your hand as tightly as
I possibly could
whilst we were hanging off the cliffs edge
Yet you let me go with a crash
Right down to the very bottom
Leaving me with no choice
But to suffocate in my own heartbreak.

You Do Not Deserve To Be Mine

I was blinded by your affection
The way you would give me constant attention
Sure,
I was dying to be loved
But
I do not think I was prepared enough
I was not aware as to how much it would hurt
Some of the time,
you just acted like a total flirt
Is that the way it was supposed to be?
Living a life filled with sadness and misery
Surely it is not very bright
Putting up such a fight for someone who does
not treat me right
Are you even worthy of my time?
Or am I just battling for someone
who does not deserve to be mine?

He Was The Weed And I Was The Flower

I think I have finally realised where I have been going
wrong all this time
Every boy that has been mine was mine for the same
reason. He was always the cigarette
He was slowly and continuously
burning out my lungs with lethal love
He was scorching away at my emotions,
wilting them down one by one
It was almost as though they were limp, lifeless petals by
the end Hanging off sadly and pathetically by their stem
He was simply toxic
He was simply a poison
coursing through my veins
Tearing away at any life that was left in my body or
any character that was left in my soul
It was not love
It was torture
It was possession
You do not damage someone to prove that you care for
them It does not work that way.
He is too selfish to leave me be
He cannot stand the thought of anyone else
loving me.

Lusting After Your Love

You light up my insides like a ferocious fire
Clearly your love is the only thing that I desire
I know by now that you are no good for me
But I just cannot stop feeling that undeniable energy
 - all of that obvious chemistry
Why can I not seem to resist?
Every single time we kiss
You leave me wanting more
Craving your touch
Lusting after the taste of your lips
Feeling your hands caress the curves of my hips
You were different,
believe me
You were not like the others
It seemed to be real, true love
You came along at just the right time
Right when I needed saving
Right when I needed someone to save me.

I Was Prepared For Pain

Trying to hold onto you
Begging for your love
It was like placing both my hands
over a boiling hot bonfire
I knew I was inevitably going to get burnt
Yet
I couldn't seem to resist the temptation
Your love was the bonfire
And I was prepared to get scorched.

Am I Just Meant To Wait Around Forever?

You say that we are more like 'best friends'
But
I am not entirely sure how to feel about that
Half of the time,
we act like love-sick teenagers
Yet the other half is spent bickering
like irritated, immature school children
How do I know where I stand if one minute
you are caressing my thigh
But the next you are acting as though
my skin is made from pure poison?
It does not sound like a suggestion that clever
But
Am I just meant to wait around forever?

Happy Birthday, Ex-Lover

It is 12am
It is your birthday now
The thought of you makes my heart ache
I would have taken multiple bullets for you
But
now losing you as a lover was like being shot
Right in my heart,
right where it hurts
With the most destructive gun
There's no way I can run
I wish we could go back to the times where we laughed,
the times where we had fun
Images of your emerald eyes keep flashing in my face
You captivated me back then
They caught my attention right from the beginning
When you were by my side,
I really thought I was winning
I hope you have a happy birthday,
ex-lover
You really were a pleasure to discover.

Picking Off The Petals

When we were together
He would constantly pick apart all of my imperfections
Almost as if he were plucking the petals off
the most beautiful flower
He would pick
and
pick
and
pick
Whereas I would pluck the petals off
every daisy in the field
Constantly asking myself
Whether 'he loved me'
Or whether 'he loved me not'.

Taking A Bullet For Unrequited Love

It is quite ironic how those we love the most are those
who seem to hurt us the most
Do you not think it is kind of funny?
It is almost as if they know deep down that
you are always going to be there
You are always going to care
Whether they walk out,
and
leave you
or
whether they achieve everything you had
both hoped they would
They take advantage of your love
They take advantage of your kindness
You are made to look like somewhat of a fool
A fool that cares too much
A fool that would take a bullet for someone
who would willingly
pull the trigger.

Her Eyes Are Where Her Darkest Demons Lie

Her eyes had their own language
They highlighted all of her pain
and
all of her sadness
They emphasised her fears
The times when she experienced the most madness
Why did you make her heart break?
Why did you hurt her so badly?
Her eyes cannot hide anything anymore
She is exposed
and
everyone can see the truth
All they have to do is look inside her eyes
That is how they will see where all her
darkest demons lie.

Growing From The Pain

Thorns are currently trapping your emotions inside
Preventing them from being set free
Allowing them to quiver and hide
They have built a firm cage across your heart
They think they are protecting you,
But
let me tell you, they are not
They are not letting any garden shears break them apart
Your emotions need to be set free
Like little birds flying away from the safety of
their homely nest
Whatever pain is being hidden away
You can grow from it as time ticks on
You can become who you want to be
Flowers can bloom from your bones
Love can flourish through to your fingertips
The past will no longer be known
Everything
and
everyone you touch will feel the positivity
It will radiate through from your soul
You will become a walking sunflower
You will finally become whole.

All Of The Emotions

February 14th means only one thing
It is Valentine's Day
Normally it would not be so bad
Except this year,
I am without you
You are no longer a part of my love life
 - and I am not entirely sure what to do
You spread your wings
And
flew away
I do not even know what I am meant to say
Somehow,
I cannot quite find the words to show you how much
you mean to me
As to my heart,
you are the only one that owns the key
Ever since you walked out the door
I have been feeling numb and
I have been feeling sore
You were someone that I truly adored
And
now I am forced to face up to the fact
You are not the same person anymore.

Why Could I Not Seem To Get Enough Of You?

You were like my drug
I just could not get enough
Every time I saw you around
I was unaware of anyone else that uttered
a single sound
You have been my focus since the beginning
I always felt like in regard to my love life,
I was winning
I am not so sure that is the case anymore
You are still my drug that I am addicted to
But
I am going to have to try
And
Prise myself away from you soon.

I Will Always Be Here

I just need you to be aware that
I will always be here
You can come to me about anything
Whether it is upsetting
or
exciting
There is no need to be afraid
As my love for you will never fade
Whatever it is that you want
or
need
I will make sure you do not get treated like
a worthless weed.

You Were The Spectator, I Was The Statue

I was and still am a gallery full of pretty portraits
You were the first to receive a premium ticket back then
I expected you to have considered that as a gift
You were never a creative person come to think of it
I never noticed you admiring my photography
Staring in awe at all of the scenic shots that I took
You always turned a blind eye
Pretending you could not care less
You had your eyes
and
your mind tightly shut
I do not think you ever wanted to admire
my artistic side
I do not think you ever really wanted to
Gaze at my gallery.

It Is Final

You were what I wanted for so long
But now,
You are just the lyrics of a heartbreak song.

Home Is Two Eyes And A Heartbeat

I fell in love with a boy who had emerald green eyes
He stole my heart by surprise
When we first met,
I had no idea that he would end up meaning
so much to me
Unfortunately,
at the time,
it was not quite meant to be
As soon as I was on my own
It felt like I had lost my home
Of two eyes and a heartbeat
Home is where the heart is
hence why I loved being his.

An Alcohol Addiction

You were meant to be the one man that never hurt me
Yet,
you caused more destruction than
any other man ever could and,
you did it from before I was even born
All I can remember is you
shutting me in my room for what seemed like
hours on end
Keeping your own daughter, a prisoner
whilst you most likely drowned your sorrows in
your favourite type of poison
 – your beloved booze
No wonder all my encounters with boys
who were once strangers turned sour
Leading to me becoming involved in
self-destructive behaviours
I should have been able to rely on you
becoming my saviour
Shielding me from all the rage,
rawness, and
regrets
Caused by the one man who was
never meant to hurt me.

The Deadliest Duo

Battling with an anxious mind,
And
self-harm at the same time
is like living in your own worst nightmare
Your mind is constantly working overtime,
conjuring up ways to overthink everything you think,
everything you say,
and everything you do
If only it was as easy as to just
flick a switch
whenever you have had enough
Combined with self-harm,
 it is absolute torture
Self-harm is a form of release for most
You feel helpless, lost,
completely stuck in a rut
How do you get out?
Where do you turn?
You cannot focus anymore,
and you just want the internal pain to stop,
but it won't
so,
you feel like you have to take matters

into your own hands

You cannot control anything else in your life

But,

you can control how you treat yourself

And,

self-harm is what you feel is the only option.

Live Your Life

Face your fears
Go after your goals
Strive for success
Don't you dare let anyone stand in your way
Don't you dare let anyone determine your future
YOU are in control of your own life
and your own destiny
Do you hear me?
I know that you have your own dreams that have
been at the back of your mind since you were little
So,
do whatever you can to turn them into your reality
Choosing yourself is not a crime
It is what you have to do this time.

Your Life Has No Limits

There is a life after this crippling heartbreak
You are only just at the very beginning of your journey
And you do not even realise that at the moment
You cannot look past what has happened right now
and
that is understandable
But
you also cannot sit around forever,
feeling sorry for yourself
Hoping that your ex-lover is going to
knock on the door any second
You need to get up and out
and
act like you are not bothered
There is a whole world out there
waiting for you
to discover it
Another lover destined to be with you
and
spend their days making you smile
Watching sad films
and
eating copious tubs of Ben & Jerry's may work for a

while

But,

everything else is just going to keep on moving

You do not want to be stuck still and alone,

unable to let go of the past

There are girls' holidays,

late night road trips in the middle of

no-where in particular

traditional Christmas Day celebrations with the family

volunteering in South America, just like you always

dreamed of

billions of people at University

and

out at work waiting to meet you

your future family that you have been imagining since

you were 9 years old

All of this is out there for you to grab with both hands

and embrace

So,

don't you dare tell me that you are going to mope

around whilst you are still young

One day,

someone seriously special is going to look at you as if

you put the

God damn stars in the sky

you will feel like an ethereal God(ess),

for sure

and

if you do not,

then that person is not your certain soulmate

Just always,

always

remember,

now

and

forever

There is a life after this crippling heartbreak.

3
Encourage

Do Not Allow Yourself To Be Second Best

Why talk to a boy who picks you up and throws you
back down?
It is as though you are meant to be taken for nothing
but
a clown
Why chase after a boy who treats you as though you are
second best?
It is as though he has just gone on a dating app and
swiped left
He quite simply does not deserve your time
He seems to have well and truly crossed the line
Wait for him to start chasing you
Make sure that he feels the unexplainable pain too.

Use The Bad Times In Your Life To Grow

Flowers grow back even after they are stepped on
Keep reminding yourself of that sentence as though it is
the
lyrics to your favourite song
You have the strength to prove the haters wrong,
believe me
The whole issue is nothing more than jealousy
Use the weeds in your life in order to grow
Always try to smile
and
go with the flow.

Lights Will Guide You Through The Stormy Weather

Hold my hand, and I will lead you towards the light
I know that your future is going to be oh so bright
You may not see it right now
But,
things will sort themselves out somehow
Together,
we can get through the stormy weather
I promise I will be by your side forever.

You Deserve

You deserve someone who sets your soul on fire
You deserve someone who treats you as though you are
everything they desire
You deserve someone who looks at you as though you
put the stars in the sky
You deserve someone who would never think about
waving your future together goodbye
You deserve someone who supports you in everything
you do
You deserve someone who loves you for you.

Pick Up Your Pencil

If you are the sort of person that is often fairly troubled
and who loses sleep at night due to the irrational
thoughts
that are bubbling away in their mind
Pick up your pencil and a notepad
And start writing about these demons
Do it in whichever style you wish
And treat those tear-stained pages as though they are
your personal diary
I get that writing is not for everyone
but,
you should at least give it a go for the sake of
your mental health
This isn't an English essay
But
you never know,
it may work wonders for you in more ways
than you believe.

Have Faith In What It Will Be

Life does not always go to plan
Sometimes,
you are just left wishing and hoping
For a miracle that is
probably,
inevitably never going to happen
Sometimes
your prayers will not be answered
Because
if something is not meant to work out,
it will not
Everything happens for a reason,
they say.

Darkness Does Not Define You

Your dark days do not define you
I know that right now you feel as if the weight of the
world is on your shoulders
But,
I promise you that one day you will find inner peace
You are strong enough to overcome any obstacles
And,
handle any of the hurdles that get placed in your path
Find that strength from within and hold onto it
Have hope when it comes to your future,
have faith in what is meant to be,
and let go of what has already happened
Even in your darkest of days
I will always be by your side
Cheering you on,
and
clapping whenever you have proven yourself wrong
I believe that you are capable of achieving anything,
so
you must believe it too.

Make The Most Out Of Every Moment

You only get one chance to live,
and
that is a given
One opportunity could come along some day,
but
by turning it down in that instant
You may be missing out on that one opportunity that
will not come around a second time
You may be missing out on the thing that could change
your life
And,
ultimately
influence your future
Whether you are young,
middle-aged,
 or
elderly
You have to grab onto every single opportunity with
both hands
Do not let them slip away
Make the most of each moment in your life
and,
be grateful at the fact that you are alive,

and breathing for yet another day
Stepping out of your comfort zone is one of the best
things that you can do for yourself
And,
in favour of your future
Whether it leads somewhere or not
At least you have given it a go.

You Are Someone To Be Adored And Admired

You are a work of art
You are a masterpiece
Portrait galleries want to hang you up on display
They want to own your beauty
They want to show it off to tourists
An individual like yourself cannot be tamed
Nobody can own you
You are not a possession
You are a painting to be admired
You are an ocean to drown in
You are a fairground to explore
You are a forest to find hidden treasures in
Your beauty cannot be captured
It cannot be stored in a bottle
fit for magic potions
That is the sort that only exists in your imagination
It can only be adored and admired
You belong to nothing and no-one
but
yourself.

Do Not Let Tonight Be Your Last Night

Do not kill yourself
Stay strong
The pain you are feeling will not last long
Please resist hurting yourself tonight
I promise you,
it is possible to win this fight
You have so much strength within you
Just let it show,
let the sadness go
Smile,
smile like you have never been hurt
You do not deserve to be treated like dirt
I know you may not have had the best day today
But
just hold on and know that
everything will be okay
I will be there for you through thick and thin
Do not let the haters worm their way in
Carry on going,
please,
for me?
I just want you to be happy
You honestly can win this fight
So
please do not let tonight be your last night

It Is All About Inner Belief

When you are in a dark place
you can either choose to believe that you
have been buried,
or
planted
If you believe that you have been buried,
It goes to show that you have a negative, fixed mindset
You do not believe deep down that anything will ever get
better
You have convinced yourself that you will be stuck
in a rut forever
But
If you believe that you have been planted
It goes to show that you have a positive, growth mindset
Which is open, and willing to adapt to any situation
Meaning that you will convince yourself
that you can get out of that dark place
As you believe that this terrible time will only last a little
while longer
Before you begin to blossom from that bud into
a beautiful flower.

You Are The Brightest Star In The Sky

You may believe that you are battling with your darkest
demons right now
And,
you may not be able to see where the way out is
But,
just remind yourself that there is always a light at the
end of the tunnel
Whatever it is that you are going through,
no matter how small,
or
even how significant it seems
It will not last for the rest of your life
You have to go through the bloodiest of battles to
recognise that
You are one of the strongest soldiers
Every single person who goes through hardships is a
survivor,
and
that is a fact
It is the darkest nights,
and the toughest of times that produce the
brightest stars
and
ultimately, the bravest people.

You Deserve Only The Best In Life

Grow through what you go through
Do not allow those deadly demons to take over you
Your appearance is what people
initially notice about you as a human being
But,
that is not all that your loves ones are used to seeing
You are braver than you believe
And
stronger than you seem
All you must do is hope and dream
You will never bloom into the flower
you were destined to become
if you hold onto the weeds from your past
You deserve to have love and happiness
that is guaranteed to last.

Humans Vs. Flowers

The world works in a funny sort of backwards way if
you ask me
It is ironic how we cut,
and
kill flowers,
because we think they are beautiful
Yet,
so many of us
cut,
and
kill
ourselves,
because
we think we are not
We ignore the idea of our own beauty even
existing in the first place
It is incredibly sad when you come to think of it
Since when did things become the opposite of what they
should be?
The fact of the matter is,
humans are just as beautiful as flowers
They continue to bloom,
even after they have been stepped on
 - as do humans
They use the droplets of rain to give them strength,
And,
they use the sunlight to give them the energy to grow
Much like humans use the negativity to give them
strength,

And,
the positivity to motivate them to become
better versions of themselves
Their buds push up from the broken earth,
so that this developmental process can happen
This is proof that we must break apart,
in order to become stronger,
and
wiser
Do not
think about the people that are the same age as you
Do not
focus on what they are achieving
It is not a competition, my love
You just focus on blossoming at your own rate
It is time to encourage self-love,
rather than self-hate.

A Blessing Or A Curse

I have always been the type of girl to bare my soul
at the first opportunity that I get when engaging in
conversation
with someone new
It has become somewhat of a habit over the years,
something I do without even really realising.
I am quick to reveal my vulnerability
and
let my facade disappear
within a matter of minutes
and
I can never be sure whether that is
a blessing or a curse.
I am simply too quick at sharing my secrets with
any individual who is willing to listen
We can be talking for anywhere from 30 minutes
to
a couple of hours,
and
I will already eagerly be finding ways to
tell them all there is to know about myself,
desperately hoping for the same in return.
For me,
this means that I am allowing myself to be emotionally
naked
To me,
the true meaning is that you are
allowing yourself to be who you really are deep within
No secrets,

no lies,
no false ideations
– just you being who you really,
truly
are
It can seem to be a blessing with those people that
you connect to on a deeper level
because they are actually seeing you for who you really,
truly
are and vice versa,
which is particularly important and appreciated
as the foundation of any loving relationship.
It is seen as a gift,
a precious token of trust and truthfulness
However,
it can be seen as a curse if
the person you are becoming emotionally intimate with
is
a sinner
- if their only motive involves
false pretences.
This is when you should be wary.

and
wait
before you let down your shield of strength
and
anonymity.
You see,
people often assume that to be naked
and
vulnerable
is to be unclothed,
but
actually,
you can bare the entirety of your being
even when you have layers
upon
layers
to
cover your skin.
In reality,
we all have that deep desire within us
to want something more than to show someone our
bare body
and
to see theirs in return.
We want an emotional connection
We want to know our lovers
star sign,
birth place,
sibling count
and
their favourite food,

but
we also want to know
so much more than that.
We want to know what their
most memorable childhood holiday is,
why they spent so many nights awake until 4am during
their teenage years,
 why they are terrified of growing old,
why they want to change the world
and
how they intend on doing it
– and
everything else that there is to know
both
the good
and
the bad.
That is what it means to be emotionally naked.
Should we not all yearn to have this with at least one
person in our lives?

Your Poem

This one is for you
Although I may not know you personally,
this poem is for whoever is reading it
right here,
right now
Whether you are
young,
middle-aged,
elderly,
black,
white,
mixed race
male,
female,
transgender,
or
whether you identify as something else entirely
I just want you to know that
I completely empathise with whatever it is that you are
going through
I understand how hard it is to wake up every morning,
ready to brave the day for the 7th time in a row
I get that you do not want to fake a smile anymore,

and you are sick of hearing people telling you that it will
get better,
because
what do they know anyway?
They have not battled with the same dark demons that
you have,
so
why should you listen to them?
Coming from someone that has
struggled silently with her mental health for most of her
teenage life,
I can tell you with my hand on my heart that it does,
and
it will get better
It seems more than impossible to hold on when you are
stuck in a situation,
but
there is always a way out
Ending your life will not end the pain
Ending your life will not make things better
for yourself,
or
for your loved ones
It will just pass the pain onto them,
and

once you are gone,

they simply will not be able to carry on

Every single person on this Earth is here

for a reason,

whether they recognise it yet,

or

whether they need to be reminded on a daily basis

You were born,

and you are living,

because you have a purpose

Maybe it is to make music

Maybe it is to educate people about mental health,

and

smash the stigma

Maybe it is to smile at strangers,

And

spread that glimmer of hope

onto them

It does not sound like much,

but

all it takes is one person to make a significant difference

No matter what people around you say

or

do,

I believe in you,

and

I always will

One day,

someday,

this pain that feels oh so permanent right now,

will gradually fade away to the back

of your mind,

and memory

You are a gem,

who will never understand

their true value

But,

you just have to trust me when I tell you that

this world would not be the same without you in it

You may think you are just one individual,

but you are so much more than that

You have a heart that is fighting with every passing

moment

to keep you alive,

You have millions of tiny cells that are trying to

protect you from poison

You have a digestive system that absorbs the nutrients

you consume,

so

you can remain healthy,

and
fully functioning
Every time you hurt yourself,
whether intentionally,
or
not,
a scab will automatically form
This is your bodies way of giving your skin
a chance to heal,
and
repair the damage that has been done
Why would it keep trying,
over,
and
over,
and
over again
if you were not meant to survive?

You may be;
a writer,
a footballer,
a dancer,
a friend,
a brother

a brother

a sister,

a cousin,

a partner

Hey,

maybe one day,

you will become a mother,

or

a father

Live your life however you want to,

and do not let anyone

dictate your dreams,

or

your deepest desires

Nobody can put out the fire that burns within you

If you nourish your mind,

your body,

and

your soul,

you will flourish into a fearless fighter

Which is what you were always destined to become

since the day you were born.

Start Smiling Stranger

Blowing out someone else's candle will not make yours
shine any brighter
It will just result in them becoming
a much stronger fighter
Why would you want to intentionally drag them down?
Why would you want satisfaction out of
seeing them frown?
The world urgently needs to become a better place
That will only happen if you start regularly approaching
others with a smile on your face.

Seeds Of Positivity Make People Smile

Spread seeds of happiness in everyone that you speak to,
and
meet
Radiate positive vibes right from your head down to
your feet
Love,
and
look after other people as much as you can
You may even become each other's biggest fan
Those seeds of happiness will flourish into flowers
They will ensure that every single human recognises
their capabilities and power.

Those who truly love you do not love you for your body
They do not love you for the skin that covers your bones
They do not love you for the use
and
the appearance of your genitalia
They do not love you for any of your outer features
They love you for your warm,
captivating
chestnut
eyes
They love you for your gentle smile that
radiates reassurance
They love you for your
distinctive laugh that can be heard
from miles away
You are not your body
You are your soul that is continuously
searching for sunlight
You are the person who put the
stars in the sky
You are the words that you write late at night
when all you have is your own thoughts
You are the same vivid daydreamer that you were
when you were 12 years old
You are the same successful (wo)man that you will be

when you are 50 years old
You are every sweet smile you have ever
shared with a stranger
You are every single tear that you have ever
shed in solitude
You are every heartbreak that you endured
during your teenage years
You are every happy ending that you have
ever dreamt of.

A
LOVE
LETTER
TO
ME

Do Not Allow Yourself To Break

When you have been broken in two
Do not try to find yourself at the bottom of a bottle
When the tears will not stop falling down your face
Do not try to find solace in sleeping with a stranger
When your heart begins to collapse as a result of the
heartbreak
Do not try to create another temporary
version of the person that you are
by dabbling in drugs
Do not question his/her motives
Do not blame yourself
Do not fall apart over his/her actions
You are more than enough
And if he/she could not handle that
Then he/she simply was not enough for you

Sunflowers Are Meant To Shine

I am a sunflower
Radiating light and positivity across even the darkest of
towns,
and
the dreariest of cities
Even if tomorrow brings grey clouds
or
torrential thunderstorms
I am only focusing on the sunshine
which is the hope within this scenario
I will not allow myself to see the shadows
Summer is not a season which lasts all year round
But
I make a choice to only see the good
in the world
and
I want the love
and
laughter that shines from my soul to be felt across
Even the darkest of towns,
and
even the dreariest of cities

We seem to live in a society where everyone is scared of
being alone
Hence why we are quite literally constantly glued to our
mobile phones
Popularity is so widely lusted after in
schools and colleges
Relationships appear to have turned into a competition
Of who can find a suitable significant other the quickest
or the easiest
I will admit that I can sometimes fall into this trap
myself
But
It's been this past year, where I have had an epiphany
You are only guaranteed to have yourself throughout
your entire life
Nobody else,
no matter what they say,
has a permanent position
They can up and leave whenever they damn well please
So,
why not get used to being happy within your own com-
pany?
Loneliness and being alone are completely different
things,
you know

If the popular guy wants the mean girl,

go and take yourself to dinner

If your family starts to fall apart,

go for a walk to get away from it all

Sleep on your own,

read on your own,

travel on your own,

explore every inch of this planet on your own

It is the only way that you will become who you

really,

truly

are

Without the influence of anyone

You will create your own dreams

and

fall in love with yourself

Then

you will be able to fully enjoy the company of others

– in the right way

SOCIETAL

MISCONCEPTION

♡ self-love ♡

We are all addicted to something that numbs
the unbearable pain
It gives us a feeling that we simply cannot explain
Something that takes away all of the hurt and sadness
Our minds are no longer filled
with intoxicating madness
But
is this really the way to be?
Do these things
honestly,
permanently
take away your misery?
The real answer is no
In the long run,
these addictions leave more issues than you know
So
please,
please put down the
blade,
alcohol,
or
drugs
Go and ask some of your friends
or
family

ALL ABOUT ADDICTIONS

for a conversation
or
a hug
Distract your mind
and
take time to unwind
Do not become addicted, honey
The end result is never funny
Although this subject is still quite a taboo
Hopefully that will someday become old news

Your Daily Affirmation

Repeat after me:
I am and I have always been more than enough
I am filled to the brim with sunlight and stardust
I am going to have a positive, lasting impact
on the world
I am compassionate
I am kind
I am genuine
I am real
I will never allow another human to make me
question my worth again
I may make mistakes
But
when it comes down to it
I use my courage to own and accept them
I am not my past
I am only human
I am and I have always been more than enough.

USE YOUR PAIN AS YOUR PURPOSE

Take your broken heart and turn it into art
Those who have fought in the bloodiest of battles
are often the most heartfelt writers
Those who have dealt with the most devastation
are often the ones who take the most
beautiful photographs
Just because you have been through unimaginable pain
It does not mean you will not smile again
Use your negative experiences
And find a way to make a masterpiece out of them
You may find your smile becomes brighter
when you prove to others
that they too
can become
a fighter.

4
Experience

Travelling Back In Time

If I could,
I would
No matter how much effort it took
I would travel back in time
Just to make you mine,
and
only mine
You would hold me tight
and
keep me safe in your arms
The perfect place without a single trace of harm
We may have only known each other for two weeks
But
I did not care as long as you were there
After the holiday had ended,
it was not the same
It was nothing but a monotonous waiting game
I was hoping to talk to you even when we had parted
Due to the seeds of potential love that you had planted.

Roses Rather Than Thorns

I have come to realise over the years that
It's better to be alone as a bud
with the capability of
turning into a rose
Than to be badly accompanied by
the most harmful of thorns
With no hope of turning into someone who
has a beautiful soul.

Dominated By Another Lover

When you are in her presence
Nothing else seems to matter
You are always dominated by the thoughts that
she smothers you with
Can you not see that she is pure poison?
Coursing through your soul
Destroying your dreams
As far as she is concerned
You belong to her
You supposedly adore her
You spoil her with envious affection
Should that not be me?
Should that not be me playing with your hair?
Should that not be me cherishing you with love
and
covering you in kisses?
One day you will realise
One day you will see
All she ever wanted to do was cause harm
All she ever wanted to do was harm me

I Do Not Know What To Do About You

It is 1:26am

and

my mind is intoxicated with the thought of you

You are my drug

You are my addiction

The hardest part of it is that

you do not have a clue

What on Earth am I supposed to do?

Getting Involved With You Is A Crime

Even though I know your kiss is poisonous
I would still do anything to have your lips
pressed against mine
Who cares if it is a crime when it is the only way to
pause time?
Your infectious venom seeps into my skin
It courses through my veins
Just the touch of your body against mine is
enough to make me
go insane
It is enough to make me scream your name.

We Were The Perfect Duo

Your lips were as soft as the petals of an elegant rose
Your fingertips traced the crevices of my body
Sparking a mini firework display with every touch
Your emerald eyes took in every inch of my being,
one second at a time
Your heartbeat synchronized to create a
harmony with mine
It was as though we were a perfect duo
The truth is though,
we were the perfect duo
Nothing could ever change that...
Or so it seemed

It Was Love While It Lasted

I loved you
but
you no longer loved me so
It was time for me to realise that I needed to let go
What we had was amazing whilst it lasted
It was without a doubt love whilst it lasted
But
once we had officially parted
I knew in my heart that there was no way of restarting.

Mourning The Love That We Lost

Isn't this situation such a tragic thing?
I am mourning the death of what we had
I am grieving over our past
The relationship that failed to last
How could you do this with such short notice?
You chew me up and spit me out
It is as though I am nothing more than
pure poison in your mouth
Constantly running back to me whenever you are down
Never mind the fact that I also have reasons to frown
Everyone can see that you could not care less about me
Are you blind to the truth?
Are you oblivious to the honesty?
You do not get to control me
You are not a master by any means
And
I certainly will never be your puppet.

All These Anxious Thoughts

Fear settles comfortably behind my eyes like a shadow
They are heavy
and
they are tired
Why should I have to blink back the tears?
Why should I have to mask a forced smile upon my
face?
This is unfair
and
this is outrageous
Everyone refers to me as being courageous
But
tell me,
What is so courageous about allowing fear
to fill you to the brim?
What is so courageous about allowing tears
to spill down your flushed cheeks?
I am anxious
And
I am afraid
Perhaps the only part of me that is courageous is the fact
that I still wake up every morning and
I still give each day another chance

Hoping that
someday, one day
It will change.

On My Own

You were the first person that I fell in love with
But
also,
the first person that I fell out of love with
I thought you were going to fill me to the brim with
happiness, and hope
But,
instead
you broke my entire being, and left me to crumble,
and
fall apart
On my own
The whole situation was so tender and sore
I just could not believe that you did not want me
in that way anymore
Even though there are over 7 billion people in this
great big world
How could I possibly imagine the idea of starting over
with someone else?

Holding Onto Hope Is No Longer An Option

As much as I want to hold onto hope
I cannot help but feel like this is now beyond a joke
Once upon a time,
I was exactly what you wanted
But
that is not the case anymore
You said you do not love me
like you did before
Yet,
you are the one I will always adore.

Our Future Together Is A Mystery

Out of the two of us
I was always the calm
You were always the storm
Sometimes you set me alight
just to keep yourself warm
When it came to our fiery relationship I could not help
but feel torn
Between what we could have been
and
what we should have been
One day,
fate will provide an answer for me
But
until then
It will remain a complete and utter mystery.

My First Love And My First Heartbreak

Not only were you my first love

But

you were also my first heartbreak

When we were together,

you would make my heart ache

Whether that was through undeniable lust

Or

a lack of trust

I saw a future for the both of us

No longer is that a topic that we are likely to consider

and discuss

The beginning of our relationship was comparable to

the calm before the storm

At first,

all you did was keep me safe

and

warm

You were the human that I called home

I did not think you would ever leave me alone

Months went by and it became apparent

you were the storm

Not only did I end up alone,

But
I also ended up torn
It was time to start growing
and
flourishing on my own
Forgetting the idea of calling another human my home.

The Situation Took Me A While To Discover

I got completely tangled up in your web of lies
All I could focus on was your mesmerising eyes
You left me feeling as though I had been used,
which caused me to become confused
Yet,
you were the one who had ended up being amused
Once I had stepped aside to focus on other things
You took the chance to have a meaningless fling
Everybody knew that you were as deceitful as each other
Maybe that is why it was easy to believe you would
end up together.

For You, My Angel.

My dearest Emma
You were a complete ray of sunshine in my life
Always lifting me up,
forever making me smile
Although we did not meet
You still touched my heart in a way that
nobody else ever has
I truly believe that you are now my guardian angel
You have gained a set of wings, and
you can peacefully fly high at last
This world was never good enough for you
You are simply too precious, too perfect
I will always watch out for your
signs,
and
signals
You were one in a million, my love
I hope you smile,
and
feel proud
as you watch over me from up above.

The Power Of A Piscean

She is selfless
It means she is caring,
and
understanding
But,
this can be a devilish trait in disguise
She finds it a struggle to fall in love with herself
All her own emotions build up and
overspill,
like books on a shelf
Being selfless drains all her energy
as to others,
she is always so genuinely complimentary
She is always the first to offer a helping hand,
or a shoulder to cry on
Yet,
she is the one who falls asleep
listening to sad songs
Everybody treats her like
she is nothing more than
an accessory
They only speak to her when they feel it is necessary

But,
she is selfless,
and
that is what makes her so sweet
It is definitely a trait which she wishes to keep.

Whispering Words To You

Hearing me whisper the words 'I love you' was
like music to your ears
But,
after hearing it so many times over the years
You decided that I was not the genre
you appreciated anymore.

Behind Closed Doors

I was not created out of love I was created out of lust
Meaningless,
temporary
infatuation
It was a recipe for disaster
It was inevitably never going to last
Whoever believed that the past could be
left in the past?
Born into a bubble of broken promises,
and
actions that spoke louder than words
You were not ever love birds
Your relationship was always complicated
and better seen on the outside rather
than properly observed.

On My Own

You were the first person that I fell in love with
But
also,
the first person that I fell out of love with
I thought you were going to fill me to the brim with
happiness, and hope
But,
Instead
you broke my entire being, and left me to crumble, and
fall apart
On my own
The whole situation was so tender and sore
I just could not believe that you did not want me in
that way anymore
Even though there are over 7 billion people in this
great big world
How could I possibly imagine the idea of starting over
with someone else?

It Is Not Always Beautiful, It Can Be Brutal

They say that love is beautiful
But
tell me,
What is so beautiful about a human being in
so much emotional pain caused by another human
That they wish to end their own life?
They see no purpose to their existence anymore
What is so beautiful about a human crying
so often that they no longer remember how to smile?
What is so beautiful about a human experiencing
so many sleepless nights that they start to appear like
a zombie?
Tell me
What is so beautiful about all of these consequences?
Love can quite often destroy a person
What is so beautiful about being destroyed?

Intimacy Is Not Always Sincere

He has traced the entire map of my body a thousand
times over
No piece of skin has been left untouched
If you look closely enough,
you can see how his fingerprints have left imaginary
marks on me
Just like our love story has left scars
on my soul
Playing with my heart like the strings of a violin
The way you treated me should be looked down upon
as a sin.

Home Has Never Been A House, For Me

When I was a little girl,
I would always fantasise about going to the fair
Every time I was there,
it felt like I was returning home again
I would eagerly await to go on the pretty carousel,
so I could feel the wind in my hair,
Blowing away the fears of the future,
and
the pain from the past,
or even the present for that matter
Then there was the candyfloss,
which was my favourite sickeningly sweet treat of
all time back then it tasted like childhood,
freedom, innocence,
and
pleasure,
all rolled into one Except my Mum,
and
my grandparents
never wanted me to eat it,
because it was no good for me
and
they wanted to keep me grounded,
away from all of my fantasies

In case I got carried away with myself,
and accidentally let loose to other people that my dad
was actually the devil in disguise
Something that always brought me back down to reality
with a thump was seeing the haunted house,
looming threateningly,
and dangerously in the distance
The air around it seemed grey, foggy almost, and that
was unsettling to me, because surely that meant it
should be avoided at all costs?
It reminded me way too much of my home
situation back then,
as that's where my father's darkest demons would come
out to play, late at night,
when nobody except my Mum and I was around
in the flat
I would have visions of him being in that haunted
house,
terrorising children,
and teens
when he was drunk, cackling away at the fact that he
could intimidate them
They would all get sucked into the thrill of it,
and laugh away,
whilst secretly shivering in their seats

But little do they know,
he did not need a mask;
my Father was already intimidating enough without one
Thankfully, bright lights allowed me to remain the
carefree child that I should have been all the time,
taking me off into another world,
one where only the most enchanting fairies,
and the most captivating unicorns existed Loud music
sends shivers down my spine, and through
my entire body,
forcing me to forget my fears,
and live within the moment,
because that is all that is meant to matter when you're
merely 6 years old
Where is the magician?
He should be around here somewhere,
Maybe he can help the past vanish from my mind,
and my memory
I can build a proper home within this fairground, and
ride every rollercoaster a thousand times over Letting go
of all the hurt,
and all of the uncertainty
I will allow the Ferris wheel to lift me up high, and
keep me there,
so I can have a few moments of normality,

away from the chaos,

so for once,

I know I am better than,

and above all of that

Yet,

my home is only temporary,

as it only ever comes to town for a few weeks at a time

This is simply all a fantasy,

a figment of my imagination,

and nothing more

No matter how much I knew in my heart that I wanted

to stay I had to wave goodbye to any hope of happiness,

and say hello to the haunted house,

once again when all of the magical lights had gone out.

The Love Triangle

When she first came onto the scene
Everybody,
myself included,
thought that she possessed similar characteristics to
those of a daisy
She seemed as innocent as any other girl could be,
and
as pure as any boy could have possibly wanted her to be
but,
that was expected,
surely
Nobody knew what she was really like,
So
they could not imagine anything different
When you first got together,
You both thought it was real, true love
As did everybody else, myself included
It was a new relationship,
a new beginning
But,
did we all really expect it to remain that way for long?
Oh,
how foolish could we humans be

You see,

you and I were different from the get go I

was still innocent,

and

pure

Probably more so than she was actually

But,

it was just different altogether

I was so devoted to you,

and

our relationship, even at such a vulnerable,

young age

and

even during the

tough times,

and

the arguments

I was full of wisdom that I was more than happy

to pass onto you,

and

as time went on,

I became very wise in regard to her conniving character,

and

her menacing motives

She was never,

and

is never going to be the type of girlfriend that I was, and can be

Her 'love' is in fact

incredibly toxic,

and

poses quite a threat to you

You see,

you now regret not putting in enough effort with me,

and

not being as devoted as I was

You cannot help but

feel sorrow

over our deceased relationship

I am a rose,

and I could give you genuine, raw love

She is a daisy,

and

she is always going to see me as her competition,

metaphorically,

and

literally.

A Sinister Situation

I was 13
You were 17
You were the first male to touch me
Intimately
Sexually
You had a way with words
Techniques which were guaranteed to trick me already
tied around your tongue
I was fooled into thinking that you wanted to play a
game. That is exactly what you wanted to do
But
not in the way that I had so innocently imagined
I knew that you were the type to travel around
But
I never expected you wanted to use your hands to travel
around my body
You were simply a stranger to me
You fucked me up
You left me terrified
You left me traumatised
You left me unable to trust any other male for a very
long time
Even though you had a girlfriend

and

I had a boyfriend

You lead me to believe I could have been someone spe-

cial in your eyes. I was silenced by your sweet talk

and

blinded by your bold character

I was a fool in thinking that I could have

fallen in love with a predator

I fought a war in my mind for years,

questioning your true intentions

I did not want to accept that I was a victim of sexual

assault

I did not want to accept that I was your victim

Well, you best believe that I am a survivor

and

I survived that shit on my own

Even though getting the news that you had pleaded not

guilty ripped me to shreds

How dare I not get justice for all that you

put me through.

The Beauty Behind Brown Eyes

People often state that brown eyes are boring
Just because you cannot drown in them
like you can with those that are
ocean blue
or
get mesmerized by those that represent emerald jewels
People look into them
and
suggest that they see nothing more than mud
Dirty,
unwanted,
lacking in meaningful purpose
To those who have brown eyes
or
those who love someone with brown eyes
You will understand that they are
much more magical than they seem.

Looking into them is guaranteed to melt your heart
As they resemble the finest sample of
Cadbury's creamy chocolate
When the sunlight catches them
They are no longer a basic brown

They carry hints of honey and hazelnut
Looking into them is like looking into a faraway galaxy
At first glance,
you are still at the centre of the Earth
But
after that,
you are whisked away into
a whole new world.

Always Choose To Be A Leader

Growing up means inevitably travelling along
a rocky road
People always say your teenage years are the
best years of your life
And whilst they may include some of your highest highs
I can guarantee that they will also include some
of your lowest lows
We are constantly told that our concerns are due to our
raging hormones
We are continuously told by our elders that we are
too lazy,
too young,
too immature,
too irresponsible
too much of this
and too much of that
We are the underestimated and
the misunderstood generation
So much pressure is placed upon us to portray the per-
fect appearance
Alongside the perfect personality and the perfect lifestyle
Unless you are society's idea of this supposed perfection
Then you aren't necessarily considered to be as worthy

But the real question here is, what even is perfection?
Who decides and dictates the rules?
If irrelevant strangers think that they can control the
way you live
You must do whatever you can to go against them
Ignore the trends and what others consider to be
the 'in thing'
It's better to be a shepherd than a sheep –
remember that.

Acknowledgements

I genuinely do owe eternal gratitude to everyone that has touched my life in a significant way over the years. Whether you are still in my life now, and have made your way to the end of this debut poetry collection of mine, or whether you walked out of the door back in 2013 when I started writing, and edging into adolescence. I'm equally grateful for those that broke me, as I am for those that have made me.

First of all, thank you to my family. Thank you to my Mum for always looking after me, and putting my needs before your own. You have my best interests at heart, and you have always done what you can for me. I don't say it enough, but I appreciate your efforts, and how you have never left my side. I know I haven't been the easiest of teenagers to raise, but I'm sure you will agree that I do have my positive points too. I think it's insanely courageous of you to raise me without the support of the man who is half responsible for my existence, but it just goes to show that you're more capable than you probably ever thought you would be. Whatever idea I have, you always listen to it, and get on board, even if you worry about the logistical side of things. I know that, deep down, you'll always be proud of everything that I've done, and all that I'm continuing to achieve.

Thank you to my biological Father for choosing to move out of the flat when I was 6 and a half years old. You have dipped in and out of my life since then as you please, whilst building your own family unit, and doing your own thing halfway across the country, but that has done me a favour. If I had grown up with a man that I could call Dad, I probably wouldn't be the strong, sassy woman that I'm now becoming. I do understand your alcoholism was something that ruled your life, and maybe it still does – who knows – but, I'm your only child, and you shouldn't have brought me into this world if you weren't going to be 100% invested in me. Having said that, what's done is done, and I've moved on with my life now.

Thank you to my sister (skin and blister!) Sophie for genuinely being the best sibling that a girl could ask for. We may not have always seen eye to eye, and in a lot of ways, we have total opposite personalities, but I think that's what makes our relationship special. You constantly inspire, and encourage me when I witness the incredible things that you're achieving. You have always been so confident, and headstrong, and that's something I do respect. I value you so very much, and I know that even though we may bicker and get on each other's nerves, we have always got each other's backs when it comes down to it.

Thank you to my Aunty Jenny and Uncle Geoff for always guiding me, supporting me in all of my endeavours, and for being so generous to me over the years. You always take me out to the loveliest of places (St Ives and Nice were both magical), and your pearls of wisdom are invaluable. You are so savvy and business-minded, and there's so many things that I could, and do learn from you each time we speak. I'm lucky to have individuals in my life, who want to spend time with me, and who want to see me do well, and build a happy and successful future.

Thank you to my Grandma and Grandad for being the best grandparents in the entire universe. Nobody else could ever compare to you as a couple, nor as individuals. You have the most beautiful, precious marriage, and it has always been such a good example for me as to what a healthy relationship is meant to be like. You have been there right from the beginning, and you have honestly made me who I am today. You are so selfless, so kind, so loving, so funny, and you really do make this family what it is. Words will never do justice for how much you mean to me, and how much I appreciate all the times you have been there when I've needed it. I feel so blessed to have been raised with nothing but encouragement, motivation, love and protection. All I ever want is to make you two proud. You know that I love you both beyond explanation, and that fact will remain true forever.

Thank you to my first boyfriend for everything that we have experienced together since I met you when I was 12. You were the first person that I experienced such intense emotions with, and there literally wasn't a single thing that I couldn't tell you. You always knew how to cheer me up, even on the darkest of days, and you supported me with all of my anxieties. I will always admire how confident and courageous you come across as to others, and I genuinely do believe that you're the reason why I'm now much stronger, and don't take any shit. I wouldn't have grown as much as I have if it wasn't for you – and I mean that in regard to both the happiness you brought me, and the heart-break you made me endure. No matter what direction our lives take us in, just know that you have been such a significant part of my journey through adolescence, as I have been through yours, but now it's time to trust that if our paths are meant to be aligned, then they will be somehow.

Thank you to my friends, both in the past, and in the present, online, and "in real life". I've never been the type of girl to find true happiness, or a sense of belonging in a cliquey group, which is why I'd rather just have my own friends that are separate from each other. Most of my past friends, I've just naturally drifted away from, but I'm still glad that they were in my life when they were, and I definitely learnt valuable lessons from them. I'm not going to mention any names here, because I'm bound to miss people out, but whether we have been close for a few months, or a few years, I love you equally, and I'm so lucky to have you in my life. You know who you are! So much love goes out to my online friends too, who I've formed really special connections with. It goes to show that distance doesn't mean anything when the love is immeasurable.

Thank you to the team at *Leaf Publishing House*, particularly Adil, for having faith in my writing, and for enabling me to turn the Intoxicated Minds manuscript into an actual, physical book that I, and others, can hold in our hands. My dream has come true at only 18 years old, and I couldn't have found a better company to work with on something so personal. Thank you to Sarah, Amy, Laurel, Laura and Daisy for creating the creating the illustrations for my book. You have all been beyond incredible to work with, and you all have such a talent for what you do. Your enthusiasm, dedication, and attention to detail hasn't gone unnoticed.

Thank you to every single person that has connected with me on social media, reads my blog, shows their support and to whoever is going to buy a copy of this book. You are a blessing, and no words will ever come close to describing how full this project makes me feel.

And finally, thank you to my younger self for everything. You have always been more than enough, and you have now proven to yourself that resilience, and self-belief can get you anywhere. You are so much stronger than you give yourself credit for, and I hope you can now see just how valued you are by everyone. I'm so unbelievably proud of you. You're now a published author, Jadey. Your dream has come true, so it's time to start helping others to heal around the world.

Illustrators

Chapter 1 - Amy Harwood

Chapter 2 - Laurel Mae Clark

Chapter 3 - Laura Jane Jones

Chapter 4 - Daisy Abena

Helplines

If any of you are experiencing any mental health or social issues, below are a list of numbers compiled to help you.

ChildLine provide young people up to the age of 18 with help and advice on a range of societal issues, from peer pressure and bullying to unhealthy relationships and self-harm. There's the option to have an online 1-2-1 chat with a trained counsellor, visit the message boards to engage with others, 'Ask Sam', which is where a couple of advice letters are answered each week, or you can ring them/send an email, depending on the severity of your situation and which you feel most comfortable with. You can also watch videos, download the app, play games, create art, or share images. Whatever it is that's worrying you, ChildLine will help in any way that they can. Call 0800 1111
or visit www.childline.org.uk.

Mind are a mental health charity, aiming to smash the stigma and stop suicide rates from rising. 1 in 4 people are believed to battle with their mental health at some point in their life, and if they aren't affected directly, they're bound to know a loved one, who will be. They want to improve the services and support available for those struggling; make access equal for everyone, help to give people choice, and be there for anyone and everyone who may need them. Their website has an A-Z page of information, helplines, an online community called Elefriends, and stories from real people with real experiences. Their info line number is 0300 123 3393 or you can text 86463. Alternatively, send an email to info@mind.org.uk. Any additional information you may need can be found on www.mind.org.uk.

Talk To Frank is an organisation, which I think is much more needed within today's society. More and more young people are experimenting with recreational drugs, and sometimes, they genuinely don't realise the implications of their actions. On the website, there's a drugs A-Z, a frequently asked questions page, what to do in an emergency, dealing with pressure, what to do if you're worried about someone, and different types of drug treatment available. You can call 0300 123 6600 or text 82111.

You can also email frank@talktofrank.com. It can be hard to talk to family, or even friends about this topic, but there is always information, and support available. Just remember to put your health first. Although it's important to have fun, you need to be aware that there is a fine line, and things can very quickly escalate. Educate yourself before you potentially give in to peer pressure.

The Mix is quite similar to ChildLine, but it's for young people up until the age of 25 instead. They are a free and confidential multi-channel service, meaning that they can be accessed through articles, videos, phone, email, and peer to peer or counselling services. You can find out more about housing, money, work and study, and crime and safety, which are topics that would be vital for any young person, especially during this period of their life. Call 0808 808 4994, contact their crisis messenger line by texting THEMIX to 85258, email them through their website, or enter a 1-2-1 chat with a specialist helpline supporter.

Intoxicated Minds
First Edition
Copyright © Jade Millard 2018
Cover art by Sarah Jane Docker

ISBN 978-1-9999552-4-3